Diq

8/15

Ian Rohr

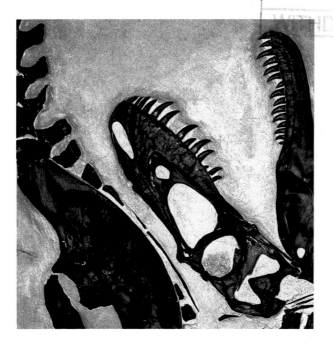

Blake
EDUCATION
Better ways to learn

Lexile® measure: 640L
For more information visit: www.Lexile.com

Brainwaves Blue
Dinosaur Dig
ISBN 978 1 86509 919 4

Copyright © 2005 Blake Publishing
Reprinted 2011, 2012, 2013
Lexile Copyright © 2013 MetaMetrics, Inc.

Blake Education Pty Ltd
ABN 50 074 266 023
Locked Bag 2022
Glebe NSW 2037
Ph: (02) 8585 4085
Fax: (02) 8585 4058
Email: info@blake.com.au
Website: www.blake.com.au

Series publisher: Katy Pike
Series editors: Sophia Oravecz and Garda Turner
Designer: Cliff Watt

Picture credits: p14 photolibrary.com; p16-17 APL/
Corbis/Louie Psihoyos; p18 Science Photo Library;
p19 photolibrary.com; p20 Transparency no.
17838-f (photo by HW Menke, 1898), courtesy the
Library, American Museum of Natural History; p26
photolibrary.com; p27 AAP.

Printed by Green Giant Press

CONTENTS

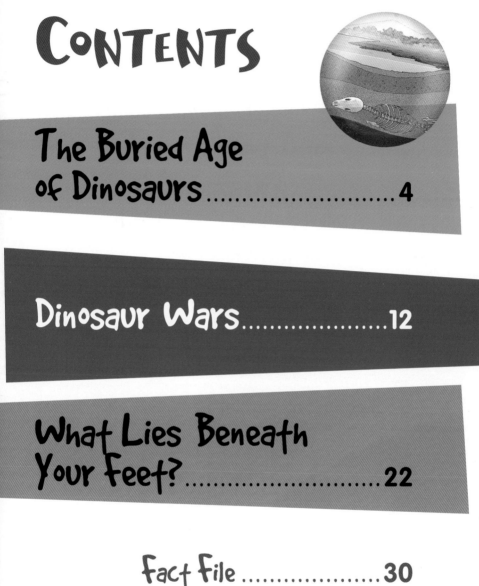

The Buried Age of Dinosaurs

Would finding something really old and very dead make you happy?

No? Well what if that something was the skeleton of a huge, meat-eating dinosaur? Or a new dinosaur that no-one had ever seen before? Sound better? Let's go dig up some dinosaurs!

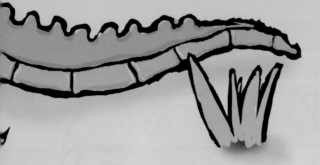

Dead and Buried

Dinosaurs ruled Earth for over
160 million years. Then, 65 million years
ago, they died out. For millions of years
no-one knew about them.

People began to collect dinosaur bones
about 150 years ago. Since then, many
types of dinosaur **fossils** have been
found. But the hunt goes on.
There are many discoveries
still to be made.

There were more than 900
different kinds of dinosaur.

Just what is a dinosaur?

Many strange creatures have been found that no longer exist. But they're not all dinosaurs. Dinosaurs were land-based, four-legged reptiles. They came in hundreds of forms. Some were gigantic, others the size of a chicken. Some ate meat, others ate grass and leaves.

'Dinosaur' comes from the Greek language. It means 'terrible lizard'.

A Passion for the Past

So what is it about dinosaurs that excites us? Is it because they were so different from us?

Q: What do you call a dinosaur that drops all the dishes?

A: A Tyrannosaurus wrecks.

Is it the massive size of some of them? A *Tyrannosaurus Rex* tooth was larger than your hand and can still cut through flesh after 70 million years in the ground!

The teeth of a Tyrannosaurus Rex

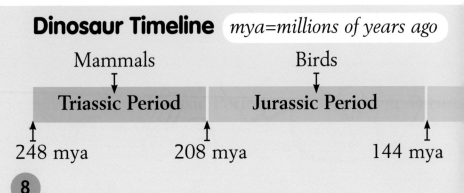

Dinosaur Timeline *mya=millions of years ago*

Mammals

Birds

Triassic Period   Jurassic Period

248 mya   208 mya   144 mya

Or is it the mystery of how they became **extinct**? Was this caused by a string of massive volcanic eruptions? Or did a huge meteor hit Earth?

A meteor crater in Arizona

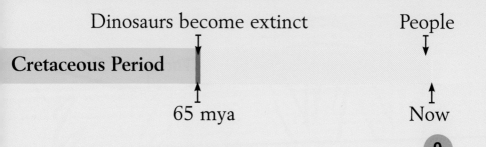

Dinosaurs become extinct

People

Cretaceous Period

65 mya

Now

Fossil Finder Top Spots

Dinosaur bones and fossils have been found from burning deserts to frozen Antarctica. But as the map shows, some places are top spots for digging up dinosaurs.

Lyme Regis, southwest England
Fossils of Pterodactyls and Plesiosaurs found at this site. A favourite spot for fossil hunters.

Plesiosaur

Velociraptor

New site

The Karoo Basin, Africa
Many Sauropod fossils found here. Some are from 250 million years ago.

Diplodocus

**Flaming Cliffs,
Gobi Desert, Mongolia**
Discovered in the 1920s.
Some of the best known
dinosaurs, such as
Velociraptors, have
been found here.

**Como Bluff,
Wyoming, United
States of America**
Remains of dinosaurs
such as the 27 metre
long Diplodocus
found here.

**Yunnan Province,
China**
Six dinosaur skeletons
were found at this site
in 2004.

Diplodocus

Valley of the Moon, Argentina
This valley is famous for
its fossils of the relatives
of crocodiles, mammals
and dinosaurs. Fossils
from the Triassic period
have been found here.

Winton, Australia
Over 3 000 footprints
made by over 300
different kinds of
dinosaurs have been
found here. The
footprints were made
95 million years ago.

Dinosaur Wars

It's easy to get it wrong when you're making a dinosaur.

Edward Cope and Othniel Marsh were both fossil hunters. Cope was proud of his latest dinosaur skeleton. He'd put it together himself. Marsh just laughed at him. Cope had put the dinosaur's head on the tip of its tail!

The two dinosaur hunters hated each other from then on.

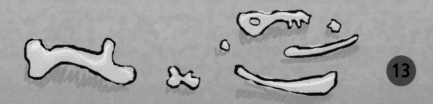

Dinosaur Kingdom, Dinosaur Graveyard

Como Bluff, Wyoming can be a tough place. The summers are hot and the winters are wild. Dinosaurs lived here in the **Jurassic period**.

Many dinosaurs were **preserved** here.

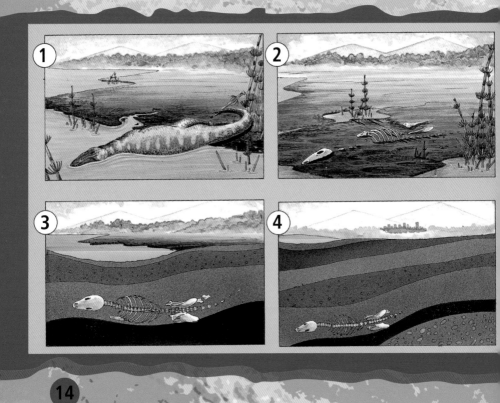

How animals become fossils

Figure 1 – The animal, in this case an Iguanodon, dies.

Figure 2 – The flesh rots away, leaving only the bones. The bones lie undisturbed, or they may be moved by animals or water.

Figure 3 – Sediments (fine soil) slowly cover the animal's remains. Over a long period of time the sediments harden to become rock. Meanwhile, chemicals in the sediment enter the bones.

Figure 4 – The Iguanodon's bones are now made up of minerals. These make the bones stronger, helping to preserve them. Erosion can expose the fossilised bones, or they lie deep within the ground, waiting to be found.

A Great Discovery

In 1872 they were building a railway through Como Bluff. Two workers cut through some 'larger than life' bones.

That's a mighty big chicken bone we found.

The workers wrote to Othniel Marsh.
They told him that their find was for sale.
Marsh had money. He sent a team to dig
straight away.

Paleontologists are still looking for bones at Como Bluff.

Battling over Bones

Marsh couldn't keep Como Bluff a secret. Edward Cope soon heard of the rich find. He too sent a team.

Edward Cope

Othniel Marsh

The **rival** gangs worked fast. They spied on each other and kept their guns close by. When a team finished at a site they smashed all the bones

My bone is bigger than your bone.

You call that a bone? This is a bone!

left there, to stop the other man's team from using them. Marsh and Cope fought a bitter war over a hill of bones.

The Upright Dinosaur

The skeleton of one huge grass-eater — the Apatosaurus — was found standing up. This giant dinosaur may have become stuck in a deep, marshy area. Then it may have sunk, like into quicksand.

19

Jurassic Jackpot

New bones keep poking out at Como Bluff. It's not dug out yet. The remains of more than 300 species of living things have been found there.

Como Bluff is a fossil hunter's treasure chest. The giant, grass-eating Sauropods were discovered there. Most of the 250 early mammals were also found at Como Bluff.

Over 20 different dinosaurs were found at Como Bluff.

Dinosaurs at Como Bluff

Allosaurus
- high IQ • meat eater
- 5 metres tall

large teeth

2 legs

2 short arms

clawed feet

Apatosaurus
- low IQ • plant eater
- 4·6 metres tall

long neck

long tail

4 legs

Ceratosaurus
- high IQ • meat eater
- 4·5–6 metres tall

horn on nose

very good eyesight

2 short arms

2 legs

Diplodocus
- low IQ • plant eater
- 5 metres tall

small head

long tail

4 legs

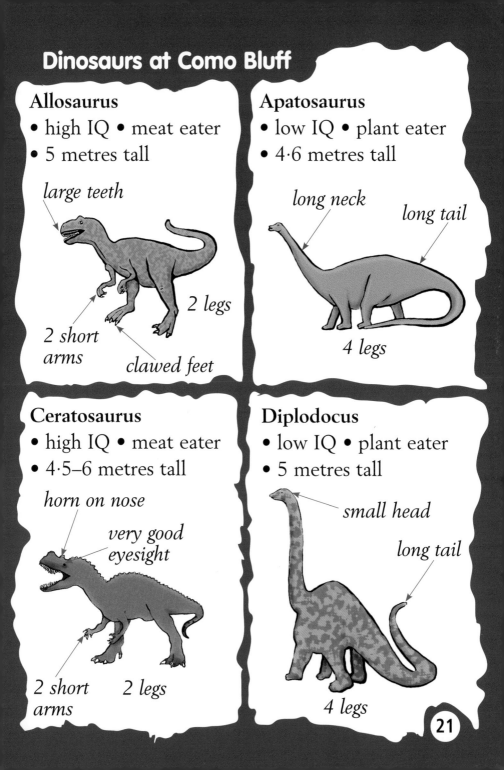

What Lies Beneath Your Feet?

It's hard to move when you've been in the same spot for 70 million years!

Finding a dinosaur's skeleton is just the start. It's a long trip from the dig to the lab. Helicopters, bulldozers and dynamite are all used to get a dinosaur back on its feet again.

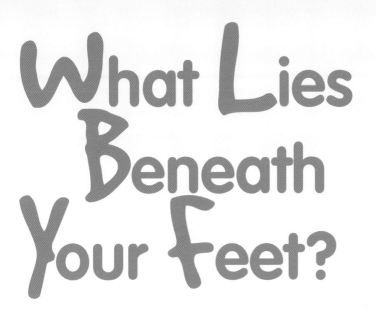

Finding Fossils

Q: What do you call a fossil that doesn't ever want to work?

A: *Lazy bones!*

You have to walk with your eyes on the ground to be a good fossil finder. Places where rocks are **eroding** might have fossils. Creek banks, dry riverbeds and cliff faces are all good places to look. But be careful! Rock falls from cliffs are common and dangerous.

What is sedimentary rock?

You can see the layers in sedimentary rocks. Each layer is made of tiny bits of rock, sand and mud. Many creatures can be preserved in the layers. Sedimentary rock is the best rock for fossil hunting.

Coastlines and beaches are good places for finding rocks with fossils inside.

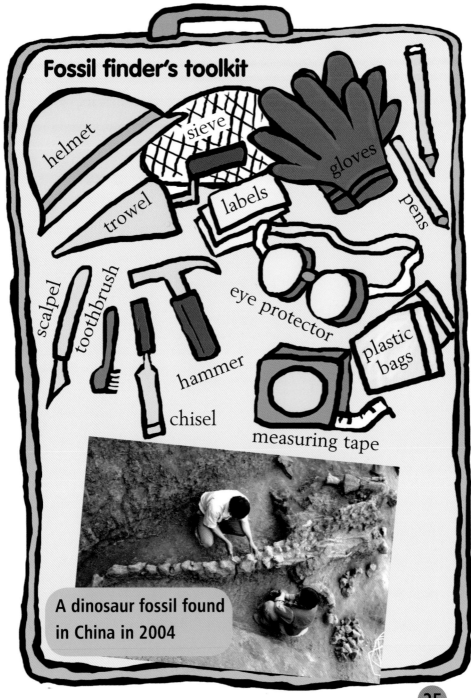

Fossil finder's toolkit

helmet

sieve

gloves

pens

trowel

labels

scalpel

toothbrush

eye protector

plastic bags

hammer

chisel

measuring tape

A dinosaur fossil found in China in 2004

Digging Out Dinosaurs

Some fossils can be dug out in minutes, others take months. Most fossils are covered by a thick layer of rock. At some sites, explosives blow up the rock and bulldozers cart it away.

Often the whole block of rock, with its bones, is cut out. This is taken back to the lab where the bones are carefully removed.

Most sites are mapped and photographed during the dig.

Bones on Board

Fossils are fragile; they are easily broken. When moving them, small bones can be sprayed with glue to stop them breaking. Big bones are often wrapped in plaster.

Too much plaster!

Giant Jigsaw Puzzles

Edward Cope wasn't the only person to stick part of a dinosaur in the wrong place. Putting one back together takes skill, **patience** and a lot of time.

Using photos and drawings, the skeleton is laid out on the floor and then put back together from the ground up.

Dinosaurs Roam Again

Movies, such as *Jurassic Park*, have recreated the world of the dinosaur. Using computers and imagination, the film-makers brought dinosaurs back to life.

Most bones are too **fragile** to become a skeleton in a museum. A plaster or plastic cast is made. It is rare to find a complete skeleton – most museum dinosaurs are put together with extra parts.

Many museums have dinosaur and fossil displays.

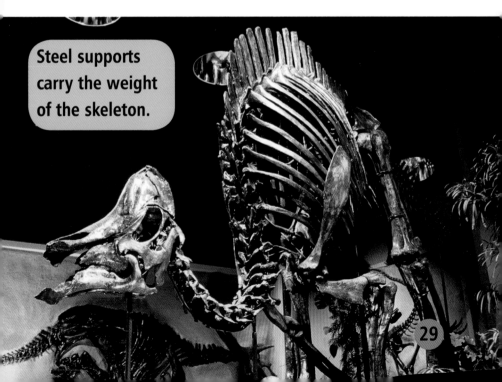

Steel supports carry the weight of the skeleton.

Fact File

My Grandfather was a dinosaur!

In a way, dinosaurs aren't extinct. Birds are believed to be descendents of the dinosaurs and some dinosaurs had feathers.

Triceratops and Torosaurus, the largest of the horned and frilled dinosaurs, were 10 metres long and weighed up to 10 tonnes. The biggest Torosaurus skulls are 3 metres in length.

Now, if I could just lift my head.

One of the largest meat-eating dinosaurs to be discovered is Gigantosaurus from Argentina. These massive munchers were nearly 14 metres long.

Better than a steak knife.